Searchlight BOOKS™

Celebrating Failure

Great Technology Fails

Barbara Krasner

Lerner Publications ◆ Minneapolis

Lerner Publications Company
An imprint of Lerner Publishing Group, Inc.
241 First Avenue North
Minneapolis, MN 55401 USA

For reading levels and more information, look up this title
at www.lernerbooks.com.

Main body text set in Adrianna Regular.
Typeface provided by Chank.

Library of Congress Cataloging-in-Publication Data

Names: Krasner, Barbara, author.
Title: Great technology fails / Barbara Krasner.
Description: Minneapolis : Lerner Publications, [2020] | Series: Searchlight books.
    Celebrating failure | Includes bibliographical references and index. | Audience: Age
    8–11. | Audience: Grade K to 3.
Identifiers: LCCN 2019017245 (print) | LCCN 2019020588
    (ebook) | ISBN 9781541583412 (eb pdf) | ISBN 9781541577312 (lb : alk. paper) |
    ISBN 9781541589339 (pb : alk. paper)
Subjects: LCSH: Inventions—History—Juvenile literature. | New products—History—
    Juvenile literature. | System failures (Engineering)—History—Juvenile literature. |
    Product management—History—Juvenile literature.
Classification: LCC T212 (ebook) | LCC T212 .K74 2020 (print) | DDC 609—dc23

LC record available at https://lccn.loc.gov/2019017245

Manufactured in the United States of America
1-46753-47744-7/11/2019

Contents

Chapter 1

A PICTURE'S WORTH WHAT?

Long lines of people waited to enter one of Bell Laboratories' seven booths at the World's Fair Exposition in Queens, New York, on April 22, 1964. They wanted to try the latest technology made by the company. They could connect with a stranger just by pressing a button marked *V* for video.

The modern white Bell System Pavilion held exhibits showing the latest communication technology.

The new Picturephone was 7 inches (18 cm) tall, 1 foot (30 cm) wide, and 1 foot (30 cm) deep. It connected to a touchtone telephone handset. The picture was black and white. People at both ends of the call had to remain perfectly still for the picture to come through clearly.

An ad for the Picturephone called it a mix between a telephone and a TV set.

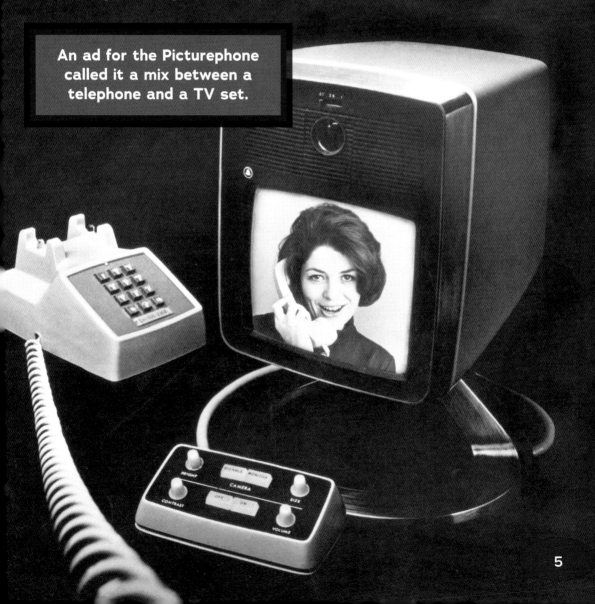

LADY BIRD JOHNSON AND SCIENTIST DR. ELIZABETH A. WOOD TALK ON A PICTUREPHONE ON JUNE 24, 1964.

▼

The laboratory's parent company, AT&T, officially launched the service two months after the fair. The company invited the First Lady to demonstrate the system. Lady Bird Johnson made a call from Washington, DC, to New York City.

AT&T was sure the new technology would be a big success. So AT&T installed Picturephone booths in buildings in New York City, Chicago, and Washington, DC. Callers made a reservation in advance to use the service. They paid $16 for a three-minute call. That's $121 in today's money.

A deaf man spoke with someone using sign language through the Picturephone.

Communicating with pictures seemed like a great idea. But the Picturephone was expensive. AT&T had invested hundreds of millions of dollars. Yet no one wanted to pay so much for the service.

AT&T tried selling Picturephone service to businesses too. They did not want the technology either. Then, in 1982, the company offered the Picturephone Meeting Service, a way for businesses to have meetings using video. But a customer had to pay more than $100,000 just for the equipment. A single call cost more than $2,000. AT&T thought businesses would accept these prices.

The first long-distance call in the late nineteenth century was one of the first steps in the invention of the Picturephone.

AT&T had poured so much effort into it, and still, no one wanted the Picturephone. It was called the most famous failure in the history of the Bell Telephone system. But the idea would later succeed. People use FaceTime, Skype, and Google Hangouts to talk through video. The internet and low-cost technology changed the way we make video calls.

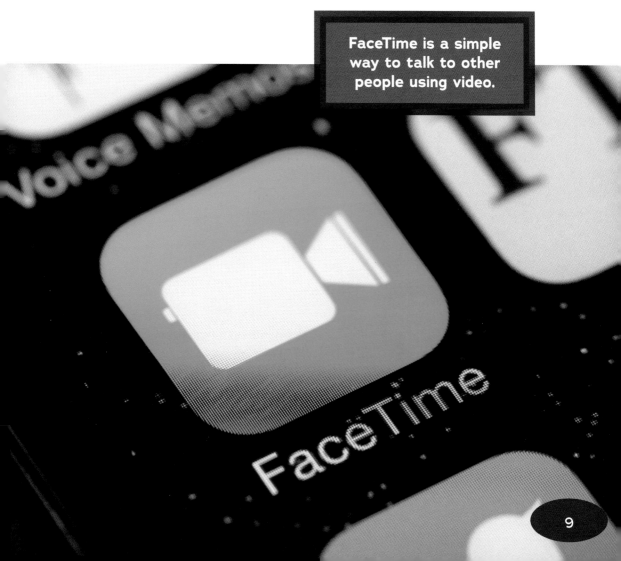

FaceTime is a simple way to talk to other people using video.

Failure Leads to Success

Failures such as the Picturephone aren't unusual or all bad. They are part of developing new technology. Each failed piece of technology teaches engineers and inventors something. They learn what didn't work and what to avoid. Many kinds of technology failed at first or took a while to catch on.

Inventor Thomas Edison failed many times while inventing the light bulb.

Inventor Alexander Graham Bell invented the telephone.

Just look at Alexander Graham Bell. He introduced the telephone in 1876, but few used one until the early twentieth century. And in the 1870s, Thomas Edison believed it was possible to record sound. He invented a device that captured sound with aluminum foil. But the delicate foil was usable only once or twice. Edison did not give up on his idea, though. Ten years later, he figured out the right technology. Then the phonograph (a record player) became a household staple.

Failing Upward

While Bell Laboratories flopped with the Picturephone, it was also responsible for major technology that succeeded. It revolutionized the world of radio in 1947 with the invention of the transistor. In 1958, Bell researchers wrote about a new technology called laser. This device creates and intensifies beams of light. Lasers are used in space exploration, surgery, supermarket product scanning, and laser printers. Bell Laboratories also developed mobile phone technology that police officers used. Bell Laboratories has received nine Nobel Prizes in Physics and Chemistry for its work.

The first transistor led to big changes in electronics.

Chapter 2

NOT READY FOR PRIME TIME

Often companies rush to get their new products into the marketplace. They are excited by their new technologies. This enthusiasm can lead to success, or it leads to failure. Products may not work as promised. People may not see the benefits. These technologies and products may have needed more testing before going public.

Apple's Lisa computer came out in the early 1980s.

A KID CONTROLS HIS GOOGLE EYEGLASSES BY TAPPING THE SIDE.

In 2012, Google introduced special eyeglasses called Google Glass. They weren't designed to help a person's eyes. They were made as a mobile internet screen. Google Glass showed the internet and used voice commands. The person wearing them could take photos and videos with a built-in, hands-free camera.

Google tried to make the eyeglasses cool. The company launched the product with a live skydiving demonstration. To promote the glasses, Google asked celebrities such as Oprah Winfrey, Beyoncé, and royal family members including Britain's Prince Charles to wear them in public. Google Glass even appeared in an episode of *The Simpsons*. Fashion designer Diane von Furstenberg used them in one of her runway shows. *Time* magazine called them one of the best inventions of 2013.

Famous people such as Prince Pieter-Christiaan of the Netherlands wore Google Glass in 2014.

Not everyone liked Google Glass.

But the glasses cost $1,500 a pair. Few wanted them at that price. People also didn't like the way the glasses felt while wearing them. After selling tens of thousands instead of hundreds of thousands of glasses, Google pulled the product in 2015. Google had brought the product out before it was ready. The team kept working on the glasses and reintroduced them in 2017. This time, they focused on selling the glasses to doctors and engineers. Google continues to look for ways to market this technology.

The Road to Failure

Google executive Sergey Brin made the decision to release Google Glass before the product was finished. He wanted technology users and journalists to try them first. He wanted their feedback so he could improve the glasses. Journalists said they had poor battery life and other problems. Restaurants and movie theaters banned the use of the glasses. They didn't want their customers recording movies without their permission. Technology reviewers called it one of the worst products ever made.

Google Glass never caught on with the public.

Learning from Lisa

In 1983, the new Apple computer company introduced a computer called the Lisa. It used a new technology, a graphical user interface. It allowed users to use a mouse and click on the screen. This opened computer screens, menus, and apps. Apple wanted to sell the Lisa to big businesses. But it had a hefty price tag of $10,000. The Lisa didn't offer enough applications to make the price worthwhile to businesses. It also didn't work quickly enough. The first model of the computer sold only ten thousand units. The Lisa was a failure.

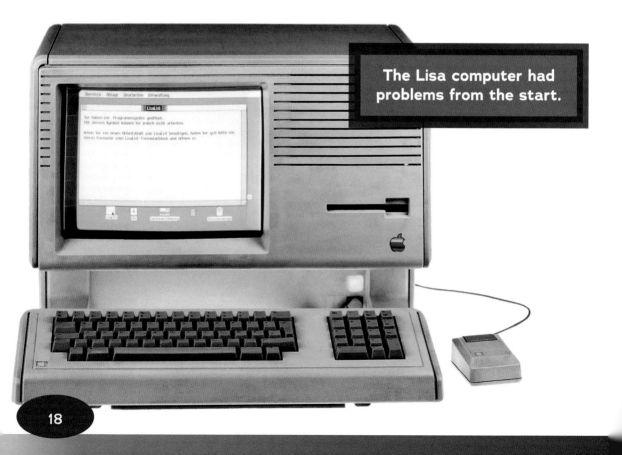

The Lisa computer had problems from the start.

But the company learned important lessons from the Lisa experience. While working on the Lisa, it was also developing a less expensive version called the Macintosh. Apple applied these lessons to this new machine. Introduced in 1984, the Macintosh revolutionized the personal computer industry. But it, too, had some initial problems. It didn't have enough memory, and users complained it was slow. Apple solved this problem in 1986, and the Macintosh became a best-selling personal computer.

Chapter 3

FAULTY SWITCHES AND BATTERIES

AT&T was known for being reliable. Yet on January 15, 1990, something went terribly wrong with its telephone service.

Many people use AT&T's phone service every day.

A switching center in North Carolina

A switch at one of AT&T's 114 switching centers malfunctioned. The center connected calls, but it had to be shut down. When it came back up, it sent a signal to other centers. They tripped, reset, and sent similar signals. All the centers crashed. What happened? A small bug was buried in more than millions of lines of new computer code. This new code was supposed to improve the call connection speed. The backup system, unfortunately, had the same bug. It also crashed.

Millions of calls went nowhere for nine hours. The outage affected businesses across the country. CBS News could not verify the story of the phone outage with local bureaus. AT&T publicly apologized to its customers. It reinstalled a previous version of the software to fix the network.

But in 1998, it happened again. Only this time, the data network maintained by AT&T crashed. It took days to pinpoint the problem. The issue was a software upgrade. Both system failures proved how critical telephones and data networks are to how we live and work.

AT&T had a second switching center problem.

Hot Batteries

Sometimes what goes wrong is software inside a phone. This happened to the Samsung Galaxy Note 7, introduced in August 2016. People liked the phone, but it had a major battery flaw. The battery caused the phone to short-circuit and overheat. This made the phone explode and catch fire. On a Southwest Airlines flight, the crew evacuated the plane after one passenger's phone caught fire. So the US Department of Transportation outlawed the phone on commercial flights.

A Samsung Galaxy Note 7 phone

Samsung issued a product recall and stopped production. It lost more than $3 billion. At least one person has sued the company. He claims the exploding phone burned his leg. Samsung hired three separate quality control companies to identify and analyze the problem. Their findings caused Samsung to improve its inspection of the phones.

The Galaxy Note 7's failures led to developing better phones.

Galaxy Note7

Phone+

Chapter 4

BOTTLE CAPS AND BIRDS

From February to May 1992, Pepsi sponsored a contest in the Philippines. Two people could win up to $40,000. They just needed to find the number 349 printed under a Pepsi bottle cap.

But a technology error caused major problems. A computer glitch printed eight hundred thousand caps with 349 on them.

People protested Pepsi in the Philippines after the company's contest went wrong.

People swarmed the bottling plants with their bottle caps. They wanted their prize. It was only then that Pepsi found out about the misprinting. The company claimed it was a computer error. Only two people with the winning number would also find a security code under the bottle cap. They would get their prize money. All others with 349 would receive eighteen dollars.

That's when trouble started. People protested. The Pepsi plant was bombed. What started as a sales promotion led Pepsi executives to fear for their lives. It took two years for things to settle down. People filed many lawsuits against the company. But the courts ruled that because of the computer error, Pepsi only had to give the two actual winners any money.

These protesters had the nonwinning bottle caps.

Angry Birds

The gaming developers at Rovio knew failure well. They'd made mobile video games since 2003. They made fifty-one games for other gaming companies. But the games they made for their company failed. Rovio was close to going out of business in 2009.

So they decided to make a game for smartphones. They considered hundreds of ideas. One idea involved a cartoon flock of birds that seek revenge against a group of pigs that stole their eggs. Rovio called the game *Angry Birds*. It was an immediate hit. As the use of smartphones increased, so did downloads of the game. Millions of people play *Angry Birds* every day.

Many failed games led to the creation of *Angry Birds*.

The Road to Failure

John Logie Baird of Scotland was unlucky. He suffered from bad health, and the businesses he created failed. But that didn't stop him from trying. He began working on sending images to a screen. He wanted to create the television. He was able to show a flickering image in 1924. Public demonstrations followed. But Baird based his technology on mechanics instead of electronics. Other inventors had greater success with electronics. The British Broadcasting Company decided in 1935 to go with an electronic system. Baird's invention was dropped forever.

Inventor John Logie Baird tried many times to make his television work.

Edison knew that failures taught him how to improve.

Fail Often, Fail Fast

Technology inventors have all experienced failures. Products may not work as planned. Software glitches can cause problems. But failure is just part of the process. Edison once said that failure is just a way to find out what doesn't work. Every company must take risks to invent new products. They experiment, try, and sometimes fail. And somewhere along the way, they may succeed in inventing a life-changing piece of technology.

Glossary

bug: a flaw in computer software

graphical user interface: computer software that shows programs as pictures that users can click on to open

handset: a part of a landline telephone that has an earpiece at the top and a mouthpiece at the bottom

laser: a device that makes an intense beam of light

Nobel Prize: annual awards given for the best achievements worldwide in physics, chemistry, medicine, literature, economics, and peace

phonograph: an early form of a record player

switching center: a telephone company facility where machines connect or switch calls

transistor: a device used to switch or amplify electrical signals

Learn More about Technology Fails

Books

Cardell, Eleanor. *Power On! Life-Changing Technology.* Fremont, CA: Full Tilt, 2018. Learn about how technology has evolved.

Donovan, Sandy. *Technology Top Tens.* Minneapolis: Lerner Publications, 2015. Use this collection of Top Ten lists to find facts about technology and gadgets.

Hamen, Susan E. *Who Invented the Telephone? Bell vs. Meucci.* Minneapolis: Lerner Publications, 2018. Find out how two inventors raced to become the first to invent the telephone.

Websites

America's Story: Scientists and Inventors
http://www.americaslibrary.gov/aa/scientists.php
Learn about two of the United States' famous inventors and their inventions.

Technology for Kids
http://www.sciencekids.co.nz/technology.html
This website offers games, science fair experiment ideas, and interesting facts about technology.

Wonderville
https://ngss.wonderville.org/studentAudience
Through games, videos, and experiments, you can become the technologist of the future.

Index

Photo Acknowledgments

Image credits: Archive Photos/Getty Images, p. 4; Underwood Archives/Getty Images, p. 5; AP Photo/Jacob Harris, p. 6; AP Photo, p. 7; Corbis Historical/Getty Images, pp. 8, 14; PSL Images /Alamy Stock Photo, p. 9; Mondadori Portfolio/Getty Images, p. 10; Archive Pics/Alamy Stock Photo, p. 11; SSPL/Getty Images, p. 12; ITAR-TASS News Agency/Alamy Stock Photo, p. 13; Michel Porro/Getty Images, p. 15; Sean Gallup/Getty Images, p. 16; PA Images/Getty Images, p. 17; INTERFOTO/Alamy Stock Photo, p. 18; Oleksiy Maksymenko Photography/Alamy Stock Photo, p. 19; LightRocket/Getty Images, p. 20; John W. Adkisson/Getty Images, p. 21; Carol M. Highsmith/Buyenlarge/Getty Images, p. 22; Adam Gasson/T3 Magazine/Getty Images, p. 23; Iain Masterton/Alamy Stock Photo, p. 24; The LIFE Images Collection/Getty Images, p. 25; ROMEO GACAD/AFP/Getty Images, p. 26; Felix Choo/Alamy Stock Photo, p. 27; MARKA /Alamy Stock Photo, p. 28; Keystone/Getty Images, p. 29.

Cover Images: Serg036/Shutterstock.com; Rawpixel.com/Shutterstock.com.